C000089116

A New Identity

A New Identity

All rights reserved. No part of this work covered by the copyright herein may be reproduced or used in any means – graphic, electronic, or mechanical, including copying, recording, taping, or information storage and retrieval systems – without written permission of the publisher.

First published by Griffin Lore, 2024
chris.griffinlore@gmail.com

© Copyright: Chris Griffin

Typesetting and cover design by The Book Typesetters
hello@thebooktypesetters.com
07422 598 168
www.thebooktypesetters.com

The moral right of the author has been asserted.

ISBN 978-1-7394306-1-0

A New Identity

Verses for a happier life

Chris Griffin

By the same author

A New Attitude

This book is dedicated to fellow travellers in life who are looking to be 'more' than they are right now.

Ways to sustain a new identity (because it's not easy!)

You can hide a new attitude, but a new identity draws attention, some of which might be most unwelcome as others try, whatever it takes, to draw you back into your old identity.

Forewarned is forearmed. Be ready for challenge as others react to your moving on.

You will be preoccupied with finding yourself, so it helps to have a safe space.

The more the merrier. Share the book and discuss it with others who are equally curious.

Identify others who are sympathetic to your endeavours. Even better, find those who are seeking a new identity themselves.

Support groups are essential for your wellbeing, as you transform yourself, until you become more confident in your new identity.

Do not be drawn into defending your changes, just be yourself, no need to fight or to justify. Have the courage of your own convictions, difficult though that may be.

Good luck.

Contents

Introduction

What stands in the way of a new identity?

These verses speak to your heart. They may *feel* completely right, yet be challenging your mind. So, you may need to allow yourself to rebel against your mind.

It is essential for our wellbeing that we question ourselves, the way we behave and think. In the process, we may discover that we would feel happier and more at ease being someone else entirely!

When I speak of rebels, I speak of those who are willing to leave the past behind to become new identities. It is not easy as minds and egos do their very best to stop this, by telling us that we can't escape our pasts and just move on. That we do not need to rebel against who we are.

So, these verses require you to silence your mind and your ego to *feel* the message of the verse. It is then your choice whether to go back to your old, familiar identity, or whether to become a rebel who steps into a new identity.

Progress is made by asking questions. Real progress is made when we are willing to question absolutely everything, even the seemingly sacrosanct. I tried it, and it worked unbelievably well for me. So these verses dare you to do so too.

Loving Yourself & Others

In future, never sacrifice your identity for the benefit of another.

Patterns

The same old same old
Life repeating itself
Same patterns, same mistakes
Same risks of heartache
Why?

Same old comfort blanket.
It is whatever feels familiar to us.
It might not be rewarding
But why expect anything different?
Old dog, new tricks
How can that be?

We think it is who we are
When it is only who we were.
Life has moved on.
Allow it to do so
And don't fear changing with the times.

Second Chance Relationship

'The triumph of hope over experience'
Often said in a cynical fashion
When we are judged to be repeating
The same bad choices
We made in the past.

But hope is good is it not
And surely everyone
Must be allowed to change?
To respond and behave entirely differently
To their shoddy and disappointing past.

Well yes, that is so
But nevertheless
It behoves us
To take heed of red flags.
Which might clearly indicate
That such a big change
Is not yet ready to be a reality
And hoping for it only delays
What is still unfortunately
The undesired inevitability.

Better to cut losses sooner than later
And give yourself a pat on the back.

You made space for change
But kept a clear eye
To check that your hopes
Were actually valid
And not just the result of wishful thinking.

You cannot do any better than that.

Forgiveness

It is easier to forgive another
Than it is to forgive ourselves.
What grief we cause
By berating ourselves.
We should have known better.
We were taken for fools!
Why were we so stupid
So naïve and so gullible?

So
We are not perfect?
Join the club!
We can punish ourselves
Forever and a day
For so stupidly being mere humans!

Or, we can accept
That we are, in fact, only human
And forgive ourselves
Whatever faux pas
Of which we consider ourselves
To be guilty.

The past can't be changed
So forgiveness is necessary
If we are to successfully move on.

If we aren't to remain
Mired and stuck
In the same old painful memories
That make us shameful or angry
Or just very sad …
And what is the point in that?

Do we really believe
We don't deserve to move on
That instead we deserve
A never-ending loop of despair
No hope in sight for anything else?
Do we really think so little of ourselves
To wish such despair on our future?

The past may be ruined
But we still have the choice
Whether or not our future is too.
Without our forgiveness
What option is it we choose?
We choose to ruin our future
As we did our past.
Are we really such a masochist at heart?

Better we see it
We get the point.
The point is the lesson
Not getting stuck in the mire.

Of course we may hope
That we will do better
But there is no guarantee.

It might take quite a few goes
To get it just right
Where right is not perfect
But it feels it is right.

It is fine to be human
Because we are, well, a human
And we need not ever
Deny ourselves that.

Enhancement

Do you love an image of me
The outward appearance
My looks, my manners, my education
Or do you love me?
The me in the round
With opinions and dreams
Of where I am going in my life.

In fact, are you interested
In my life at all
Or only in how
I may enhance yours?

I Do Love You!

Anyone who finds themselves
Repeatedly having to say the words
'I do love you'
In order to reassure another
Must question
Whether they speak the truth or not.

Real love is expressed
As a feeling, not in words.
Words are unnecessary
When compared
With the strength and the depth
Of the message conveyed
By the feelings so freely shared
If they are genuinely
And mutually felt.

So, to be asked
'Do you love me?'
Is a red flag.

It might be profound insecurity
On the part of the other
Which is for them to confront.

But what if it means
That maybe you don't
The other knows that
And seeks to be told
They are wrong
To have such unwelcome misgivings?

Is it fair to say
'Yes I do, of *course* I do!'
Whilst blaming the insecurity of the other
For repeatedly requiring reassurance?

Perhaps it is they who see the truth
And it is you who are in denial.

Subsumption

A relationship requires sharing
Compromise and respect
All without succumbing
To the inherent risk
Of being subsumed
Of losing one's sense of self
Or of requiring the other to do likewise.

A Promise

Please don't suffocate me.
Let me be me
Let my individuality express itself
Without censure and judgement from you.

Love me for who I am
For I need to be me
And I promise
That I will not judge you
For being who you are too.

It Isn't Worth That

One choice will make us happy
Bring excitement and joy
The other will weigh us down
Be onerous and wearisome.

So why are we so often compelled
To make the latter
Decidedly unappealing choice?
It doesn't make sense
When fully exposed
To the bright light of day!

No
There must be something more at play.
Who chooses to make
Their own life more burdensome
Unless, unless …
Ah! Yes …

Let's peel back the layers.
What fear or guilt or shame
Or misplaced sense of duty
Is causing us
To right royally mess up
Our own sweet chances of happiness?
Expose that to scrutiny
Discover what is lurking
So deep within ourselves.

Do not say we have no choice
Because of this or that.
We all have choice.
The choice to be happy or not
Is ours to make
Unless we are allowing
Some fear, guilt, shame or duty
To get in our way.

If putting another first
Does not make us happy
(And so very often it doesn't)
Don't be ashamed
For acknowledging that.
Maybe instead
Accept that it's time
For some deep soul searching.
Is this really what our lives
Should be all about?

Believe me
No-one deserves a short straw
And no-one ultimately
Will ever thank us
For messing up our own
Potentially wonderful lives.

We will only have ourselves to blame …
And it isn't worth that.

Last

Do we deserve to be happy?
Oh yes, we say
Before sabotaging ourselves
In spectacular fashion!

The *ifs* and *buts*
The *shoulds* and *shouldn'ts*
The duties and cares
All getting in the way.
On top of that
As if anything else
Might even be necessary
Our guilt and shame
Put the lid on it all.

When even we
Put ourselves last
Why then, are we surprised
When others just copy our lead
And put us last too?

The Rough with the Smooth

I have to let you be you – irritating habits and all!

Perhaps perfection is acceptance of imperfections.
Letting go to keep close
Silencing criticism
Taking the rough with the smooth
Enjoying what you can
And allowing the rest to pass you by.

Let it be enough that on balance
Togetherness is better
Than losing each other.

But remember if I live and let live
Then I will ask for the same in return.
You must allow me to be me, too
Irritating habits and all …

Revisiting the Past

Life has a forward trajectory.
Reminiscing, longing to go back
To revisit the past
Is like battling the flow
Swimming upstream
To rediscover what?
Past happiness, past love
Past experiences?

But you cannot step into the same river twice
So if the past can even be reached
The pattern may be the same
But the experience will not.

Life has moved on
It has moved forward
So the old experience
Can never be recreated
However much we may wish it could.

Instead we block our forward momentum
Like water that is blocked
Becoming stagnant and foetid
So too will our lives.
Do we really want
Our lives to become
Similarly stagnant and foetid?
Put like that, the choice appears to be clear.

The question is, are we really ready
To see that rather inconvenient truth?
To let go of the past
Thank you and goodbye
I had a really great time
But I'm looking for more
So I regret to say
I can't revisit my past.

A Half of a Life

Relationships
What a minefield!
Does a relationship
Benefit both parties?
Even that question is a minefield.
Because what do I mean by 'benefit'?

Am I talking in the material sense
Of comfort, security, wealth
Or in the emotional sense
Of joy, happiness, contentment?

So many of us believe
That it is imperative
To ensure our material benefits.
We are willing to sacrifice
Our emotional benefits
Just to stay safe and secure.

We imprison ourselves
Without even being aware
That that is what we are doing.
And we can do it
For years and years …

We smile and laugh
And gradually switch off
That part of us that makes us
Feel fully alive.

We put on a show and deny
What is really going on
To ourselves
As well as to others.

Does it matter?
We made our choice
It is our duty to uphold it
And we are so safe and secure ...

Well, take it from one
Who discovered a truth
Such a relationship
Provides only half of a life!

The other half
That brings real joy
Real happiness
Real contentment
Withers and dies
Whilst we attend to our duties.

Now, really, in the cold light of day
Does anyone ever deserve only half of a life
Security or not?
The choice is yours.
It may be quite tricky perhaps even scary
But you owe yourself
The right to ponder that question
If nothing else.
Good luck!

Upsetting the Status Quo ...

... so that your new identity can thrive!

Academic Exercise

It's so easy to pay lip service to change
To understand intellectually what needs to be done
The hard bit is how to embody that change
To live it, to breathe it, to truly embrace it.
But until we do that
Until we truly believe
Our ability to change
Will forever just be
An academic exercise
And never any more.

Identity

Your identity is an entity
An image created by you.
Even the name explains its purpose.
It is the ego
Nurtured and developed
And so has nothing to do with you –
At least the real you behind the ego.

We nurture and protect
Our individual identity
For much of our lives, if not all
Until we realise
That it is but a mask
Behind which
We keep our real selves hidden.

It is useful as an interface
Through which
We interact with the world.
But interfaces need updating
If they are to continue
To be useful
And reflect how we've changed
Our progress that lies behind them.

The real test in life
Comes with having to recognise
That it is our identity, our interface
That holds us back.
It is blocking and stymying
Any hope of real growth
And must be ditched
Or at the very least recognised
For what it is, or what it is not
In order to move on.

'How acceptable is that concept to me?'
'How do I get it done?'
These are the questions
We might ask ourselves
If we really want
To start afresh
To be more content with our lives.

That's a Big Question!

Identifying with an existing identity
Requires attachment to that identity.
It requires focus and attention
Towards upholding and maintaining
That particular identity.
In short
It requires us to stop the flow
The chances of becoming more
Than that particular identity.

Even if you can see beyond
And can welcome a constantly evolving
Sense of identity
It is others who want to keep hold
Of your old identity
The identity that is familiar to them
And with which they feel comfortable.

And when they cannot find it
It is anyone's guess
Whether they will accept
Or even like your new identity.
And even if they do
Will they accept the loss of that one too
When time comes for you to move forward again?

So, there is the real challenge
Of non-attachment to identity.
Are you ready for non-attachment
To your friends and relationships too?

Let Go

Let go of the rigidity of control
The inflexibility, the tunnel vision
The risk of breaking, of shattering
When the fates work against you.

Let go, relax, become pliable
Be like a willow in the wind
Able to bend and absorb
The shock of change.
To spin on your heel
And set off anew
With every day a blank canvas
Ready for glorious happenstance to be portrayed.

It is exciting as you work through the fear
Of not knowing what life has in store
And trust is required that all will be well.
I do not say it is easy
But it is so much more fun
As you find yourself venturing
So far beyond
All of your previous boundaries ...

I hope I am selling this version of life
As I would like you to share in my joy
Of living a life so completely brand new
That I used to believe wasn't possible too.

Your Truth

It is for you to decide
Where your truth lies
There are no *shoulds* or *ought tos*
It is whatever
Feels right for you
Right here and now.

Likewise
It is for others to decide their truths
And it is not your job to try to dissuade them
If their truth differs from yours.

Live your truth by example
Leave others to decide for themselves
Whether living by your truth
Might indeed make them happier …

One Truth

So, your truth
Is not the same as mine.
This may not matter
Unless of course
Your truth requires
That your truth
Is the one and only truth
And that everyone else
With different truths
Has yet to be converted
Has yet to see
The error of their ways
Has yet to see the light.

So, as an example
A rather important example ...
If you build your life around a truth
That all can ultimately
Be understood by the mind
And if it cannot be proved
Ergo it is wrong
Then you will perhaps
Not respect or accept
Those who see life quite differently.

Those who believe
They don't need to understand.
Their intuition is sufficient.

Those who very happily trust the unknown
And are absolutely willing to go there
As fearlessly as they possibly can.

Whatever your truth
Do you feel thwarted
Or perhaps even quite angry
When someone else
Does not bow to your truth?

Stop struggling
And rest assured
For there is indeed one truth
That applies to each and every one of us.
It is that our truth
Will always be
The right and perfect
Truth for us …
But only for us.

Struggle only happens
If we require
Another's truth
To be a clone of our own!

Emperor's New Clothes

It may be uncomfortable
When people ask those awkward questions.
When people refuse to go along
And simply accept the status quo
Effectively
Refusing to be one of the crowd
Who marvels at the emperor's new clothes.

It may be uncomfortable
When institutions with their rules and judgements
Are questioned.
When more justification is required.
Especially when no additional justification
Ever seems to be sufficient.
When what is demanded
Is a complete overhaul
A starting afresh
A refusal to just start from here
And tweak and tweak and tweak.
All just complicating
The already complicated ...
All just adding up to a more complex system
That still just does not work.

No, the original assumptions
Are what should be in question.

And that is scary and for so many
Who are invested in the existing
So absolutely impossible to do
Without threatening their comfortability
And perhaps even their credibility too.

So, do not look to those in the know
To actually know what is best!
It will, more than likely
Be a complete outsider
Who is able and willing to see or not see
The emperor's new clothes
In all their glory!

An outsider who is also brave enough
To help more and more people
To believe their own eyes
To trust what they feel
About the emptiness of so many institutions.
That may not need to wear clothes
But are still dressed up with illusions
To dupe and control the people
By claiming that they know what's best.

Radical Transformation

We may choose to believe
We are who we have always been in our past.
But are we right to feel so limited?
What if we choose to believe
That we are able to change
Absolutely everything about us?
Our beliefs, our attitudes
Our dreams and aspirations.
The way we live our daily lives
Where we live
What we spend our time doing
And with whom we spend our time.

Do you believe such radical change
Is totally impossible?
Well, so did I, until I did it!
So now I do believe that it is quite, quite possible.

It was not my first choice, I must admit.
Life fell apart, at least my old life did.
My choice was to say, 'Enough is enough!'
To throw everything up in the air
Ready and willing to see what then happened.

Because the choice I had was to build afresh
Or wallow in self-pity
To start afresh I have to say
Was the better choice to make.

The secret now is to not hold tight
To this brand-new version of me.
To not be in fear of even more change
And to continue to feel excitement
About who I can yet become.

For the full extent of my transformation
Will only be limited
By the full extent
Of my willingness to keep embracing change.

Hidden Rebels

There are many potential rebels
Who spend their lives pleasing people
Without even realising it.

It starts as a child
When to be considered good
Required living in a certain way.
If rebellion was attempted
So life could be lived
In a way that felt more natural
Censure and punishment
Was the very quick result
Along with pressure to feel shame
About even considering
Any alternative points of view.

Far easier to learn that being natural
Did not make for an easy life
And really was not worth the pain
The disapproval, the distain.
Easier to become 'someone else'
A good child, one who is obedient
Who follows the rules
And fulfils others' agendas
As to what a successful life should look like.
There may be the odd rebellion or two
But often too brief to set a new habit.

And eventually memory fades
Of the real nature of the self
So embedded is the habit
Of the necessity of pleasing people.

It might even be decades
Before that niggle is acknowledged
That one feels a fraud
That this life that was supposedly yours
Is not in fact your life to live.
But, even then, that is just the start
Of what can be a very lengthy journey.

To accept that you are not
Who you have become
Does not mean that you can remember
Who it is that you are!
It is not easy to rediscover yourself
Under the layers and layers of conditioning
To remember who you really are at heart.

It takes time
And determination
A lot of trial and error
Unless you can listen to your heart.
What really excites you?
What particular brand of *madness* is it
That makes your heart sing?

Remember, the real you
Might be deemed to be quite a rebel.
There has to be a reason
You were so silenced as a child!

But rebels must start to remember
That they have a very important role to play
In questioning and holding
The embedded status quo to account.

If such is your calling
Give it a go
Be real and find your true friends
Those who do not feel so threatened
In the presence of rebellious people.
Spend time feeling your way
Into your new identity
That has been waiting
So patiently for you to find it.
Has waited so patiently
To bring you great joy.

Adequate

We are all equally adequate
It is just that some of us
Don't yet realise it.

We imagine we are not
And give ourselves hell
As we berate and criticise
All our own efforts.

Until we are able to see
Our own very valuable worth
Life will not be able
To offer us its best
In terms of fulfilment and joy.

Gender Labels

We are unique, every single one of us.
Best encapsulated by
A postcard I pinned on my wall
'You are unique, just like everyone else'.

But we seem to have need
To reduce such uniqueness
In order to fit into limiting labels.
Labels that then link so neatly together
With their associated
And limited set of attributes.
Some minds struggle and resist
Any suggestion
That life really isn't that simple.

Life is messy and glorious
If we are true to ourselves.
We are who we are
And if the hat doesn't fit
Then embrace the one that does.
It will suit you regardless
Of what others say
And you will feel empowered
Which is always a good start
When it comes to forging
Your own unique path in life.

The way will not be easy
As intransigent minds fight against you
But the alternative is worse
As you try hard to deny
Who you really are at heart.

Rebellion

Rebellion driven by ego is disruptive
In a way that benefits
Primarily the ego
And often only a few
Particular egos at that!

Rebellion driven by the heart
May be equally disruptive
But in a way that benefits all.
Except those who see their
Limited visions
Crumbling before their eyes.

It is what motivates
Rebellion that matters.
Who it is who will
Ultimately benefit
Not the act of rebellion itself.

Recognising What's Damaged
Part 1

If we can't see damage in ourselves, we can't sort it.

Damaged

We are all damaged
One way or another.
It is our willingness
To admit to our flaws
To accept all of ourselves
Which allows us to fully embrace ourselves.

To fully embrace and so work through
All that we fear and that holds us captive.
To find our strength and to see beyond
To pierce the veil that keeps us in thrall
To find our contentment
And become quite, quite fearless.

Go on, it only takes one step at a time
And a trust and a belief
That all is just fine.

Blame Game

It is our beliefs that limit us.
Our beliefs about our abilities
The value we place upon our worth.
No matter the genesis of our beliefs
Which will, more than likely
Be convoluted and complex
With many layers and experiences
Supporting their so-called validity
At least in our minds.

No matter to any of that
Start from where we are.
Define our beliefs
Don't waste time apportioning blame
As only we have decided to limit ourselves
Whatever another might have done.

I know that sounds harsh
When the easiest route
Is to believe we had no choice.
But we all have choices
And as I said at the beginning
It is our beliefs that limit us
Including our choices …

So, face our own beliefs first
And then, the very next step
Forgive ourselves for not being perfect.

Don't fall into the trap of blaming yourself
In lieu of blaming another.

We all make mistakes, some are even quite big
But all can be remedied in time.
It might be hard, it might be a test
We would have done it already
If it was going to be easy.

But keep going
If we want to regain our excitement
And a deeply profound sense of achievement.
Oh, and yes, a much happier life to boot!

World of Equals

In a world of equals
It is our fragile egos that create inequity
It is a fear of some kind that is behind the distortion.

Fear of not having enough
Of not being enough
Leads to greed and superiority.
Fear of differences
Leads to intolerance and being judgemental.
Fear of change
Of letting go
Leads to stagnation and immovable stubbornness.
Fear of missing out
Leads to impatience, lives too frenetic.
Fear of joyfulness
Leads to self-sabotage.
Fear of being disliked
Leads to lives wasted only satisfying others.

So, no wonder we are where we are
Constantly having to strive
To simply allay our fears.
Fears that are unrelentingly stoked every day
By politicians, the media, by us.
We all play our part
Whatever our line of business.

You may feel that fear doesn't apply to you
But we all have our fears
Including a fear of being seen as fearful
Of being too vulnerable
In case we devalue ourselves in the eyes of others.

Better to take the blinkers off
And face our fears
Whatever they may be.
Then we might slowly be able to start
To improve our potentially beautiful
Long-suffering world
As we recognise that we are all indeed equal
And that no-one should ever need
To feel fearful.

Differences

It is our egos
That create a hierarchy of differences
Differences that are in fact all on a par.
The need to feel superior or inferior
Is behind the scale of value and worth.

For some it is too threatening
To admit we are all the same.
The same, despite being quite different!

So, in the knowledge of that fear
Do you still need to place yourself
Higher or lower
On what is a false
Hierarchy of differences?

Pessimism

Pessimism.
Why do we indulge?
To avoid being hurt as we were in the past?
But then we deliberately exclude
The joy of anticipation from our lives.
Is pessimism worth that price?

Suitable Pride

If we don't love ourselves
Take pride in ourselves
Why are we so surprised
When no-one else does either?

When others can clearly see
How little we think of ourselves
They may assume that we must know best
And so they simply follow our lead.

If we are waiting for others
To love us anyway
To see something in us
We can't see for ourselves
Isn't that rather too big an ask?

If we start to love ourselves more
It's amazing
How others will see us so differently.

When we take pride in ourselves
Then others treat us much better
By treating us the same
As they see us treating ourselves!

Why Do We Need to Judge Another?

Who are we to judge another?
By what measure do we judge?
I see judgement as a need to conform
To another's particular set of rules.

But what if my rules differ from theirs?
Well, it leads to continual judgement
No common ground to be explored.

To find common ground requires
An enduring and deep-felt tolerance.
An acceptance that we are not all alike
That our lives may be and have been quite different
But that no life is then less valuable
As a consequence of that.

So it is respect not judgement
That is required
If we are ever to get along.

Valuing Self-Worth

Do we devalue ourselves first
Before others get the chance?
Do we really think so little of ourselves
That such devaluation
Is something that must be expected
One way or another?
Or maybe we have learnt to think so little of others
That we don't expect them
To recognise our skills?

But what if we are good at something?
Why should we not be proud of our skills?
It is all too easy to let a fear
Of inadequacy get in our way.
Or is it even a fear of the inadequacy of others
That we allow to mess with our worth?

No-one is second class in a world of equals
And everyone has their skills.
Those things that come naturally
And are such a pleasure to do!

So, do not be humiliated by anyone
Who is so needy they must be superior
Or by those who can't afford
To admit to your skill
In case it makes them look bad.

We are in a world that requires us to earn
If we are to get along
So we must not be the first
In some self-created line
Intent only on making our own lives more difficult
By selling ourselves too short.

It is not okay to be so humble
If it is fear of humiliation that is the trigger.
Stand proud, stand your ground
You are like all the others
At liberty to charge
The full and competitive going rate!

So, research and pitch your price in the field.
By all means be competitive
But do not be too fearful.
You will know which applies if you really think hard!

Sell your skills, not your cheapness.
I know it puts pressure on you to do a good job
But then that is your skill so why do you doubt?

It is the answer to that
That might be quite tricky
As it is, let's be honest
That which stops you valuing your worth.

Self-Compassion

Why do we choose
To do such a number on ourselves?
Criticism, disparagement
Whatever the form
The intention is always the same.

It is self-harm, self-abuse
Though rarely acknowledged
As being so.
So next time you find yourself
Going down that road
Call it out for what it is.

Then find compassion in your heart
For yourself
An oh-so worthy human being
Who is not perfect
But is doing their best
And for that should be applauded.

Self-Confidence

I'm not here to feed anybody's ego.
Why does anyone need to look to others
For validation of their worth?

We are worthy
So it matters not
Whether others are able
To recognise it too.
What matters is
Whether *we* recognise our worth.
What matters is our self-confidence.
So, don't show a lack of self-confidence
By demanding that others
Show you approval and deference.
Because even if they do or they don't
We need to ask ourselves
'Why does it matter?'

It is the answer to that
That will be the guide
Of whether we need
To work on ourselves
Rather than get angry
With all those others.
Those others we may deem
(Because it suits us to do so)
To be the ones wanting.

Making Space

Fear
Put simply is anticipating danger
Danger that can harm us.
Our bodies respond
Preparing us to react
To save and protect ourselves.
There are some fears that are healthy
Where physical harm could result
But this is not always the case.

Fear
Comes in many, many forms
Some clearly obvious
But many are hidden.
They have become so habitual
We are no longer aware
That they are even there anymore.
But they are active and compromising
Our behaviour
Our beliefs
And ultimately
Our wellbeing and happiness too.

Facing fears
Is all well and good
But fighting a fear
Means focusing on it

So it preoccupies and fills the mind
Becoming a force to be reckoned with
Taking up so much space in our lives …
Space that could be much better used.

Face your fears …
Yes, give them a name
Be aware of what they are.
Some can be quite a surprise
When we finally unearth them!
Then, rise above them
Make them irrelevant
The proverbial toothless tiger.

Act as if they don't exist
Distract the mind
Refuse to allow space
For fears to occupy.
Beat them by making them so small
They cease to have
Any relevance at all
In life both now
And in the future.

Facing Demons

A really big test is focusing on
What we don't love about ourselves.
Those things that preoccupy our waking moments
Be it our looks
Our behaviour
Our lack of abilities
Or whatever else springs to mind.

The hardest part
Is to be dispassionate
About whatever it is
That is our focus.
To assess it and ask
Why is it we feel
So very strongly about it?

Indeed the answer to that
Can be quite a challenge.
We are after all
Saying why it is
That we don't love ourselves!

We must find a way
To love ourselves
If we are ever to be happy.

So it is then a case
Of how to make peace
With such a deeply embedded
Source of conflict.
We may put right what we can
Up to a point.
But some things may prove
At least for now
To be quite beyond us to change.

So the question to ask is
Why then do we waste
So much of our time
In fighting and railing
Against things
That are actually unsolvable?
Things that then become our demons
Because deep down we know
Such fighting and railing
Won't do anything much
About them.

What stops us turning around
And using that time
On things we can do and achieve?
The things we don't have time for
Amidst all the fighting and railing.
Those things that will make us
Feel very much better
And, dare I say, even happier too.

Recognising What's Damaged
Part 2

If we can't see damage in others, we can't deal with it.

What is the Difference?

There are masculine females
And feminine males.
Such females attract respect
But such males are more likely
To attract much more ridicule.
Why, I wonder, is that?

Bragging

There are those who will claim you are bragging
When talking about something at which you are good.
But it is their discomfort
That makes them feel bad
When hearing you speak
About your successes
Even when praise is so very well deserved.

It is for them to explore the source
Of their own uncomfortable discomfort
Not to shut you down
In order to make them feel better.

Class Privilege

You either have it or you don't
And there's nowt to be done about that!
By birth or by upbringing
Either result in a natural exudation of class
It is the basis of much disconnection
As everyone searches for a niche
Somewhere that is comfortable
And where they feel at home.

Those with class may take it
And its benefits
Very much for granted.
Those who don't may constantly aspire
To gain entry to the club.
There are others though
Who wouldn't be seen dead
Anywhere even closely related!
All are embracing some version of snobbery
Whichever side they are on.

So is class beneficial
Or an outdated construct?
In a world that is equal
It should be quite obvious
But it seems it is still
The preserve of the few
Who are proving to be so loath
To have to relinquish their privilege.

Rules

Rules and power go hand in hand.
If you do not have the power
You cannot make the rules
You cannot enforce your will on others
Which is, of course, what rules seek to do.

So, the powerful set the agenda
The aims to be met by the rules.
The question that is therefore of greatest significance
Is what is it that motivates those in power?

We do not say 'Power corrupts' for no reason
So can we trust that all the rules
Are not specifically designed
To favour those in power
To minimise rebellion
Where those for whom the rules do not work
Try so hard to be heard
And therefore respected?

Look only to the nature of any rule makers
For it defines how suitable those rules will be
It defines how respectful the rules are to others
It defines the tolerance and selflessness of those rules ...

In short, it helps to explain how the world
Has become so very messed up
And that will unfortunately endure
If it is only the powerful who make the rules.

Limitations

We are brainwashed into believing
There is a right way and a wrong way
With rules and regulations
To ensure our compliance.
My way or the highway so to speak.

A rebel is there to question such rules.
To point out that such rules
Are only required when we are distrusting
Of our fellow human beings.
When we believe that we know better than them
How things should work
And how they should not.
But my experience has shown me
That rules tend to tighten
As the powers that be
Seek to control
To stem rebellions.
Ultimately even trying to stem the tides of progress
That inexorably carry us forwards.

So, I see there are losses when enforcing such rules
Even rules set with the best of intentions.
Such rules will have some element of gain.
But when gains are small
When compared with the losses
Then it is the rules themselves
That are the problem.

And at their worst they will hamper progress
And stop advancement
Stone-dead in its tracks.

But to send that message
Requires a loud enough voice
And those who still trust
In the inherent goodness of others
In humans who do not need to be governed
With such an iron fist
To ensure they do good not harm.

So rules are borne of fear
Of doubting the goodness of others
Of not having faith
That fellow human beings
Can create a world that works
Perhaps with a more expansive plan
Than any plan envisioned
By the rules.

Because rules by their very existence
Are intent on setting
Specific and strict
Man-made limits.
Limits that are set
By a limited set of limited minds.

How much more limitation can you possibly get?!

Toxicity

What is toxicity
Toxic thoughts, toxic behaviours?

It is behaviour and thinking
Borne of fear.
Some fear that's unacknowledged
But powerfully
Compelling us
To act in a way
That harms our wellbeing
And also so often harming
The wellbeing of others too.

If you are on the receiving end
It helps to remember
That whatever they say
It is really not about you.
You are just a trigger
That requires them to go
Into their protective mode
To hide their vulnerability
Whatever that may be.

It seems like a force
A strength to be reckoned with
And will require you
To consider it as such.

By doing all that is necessary
To protect yourself
Even though the reason it exists
Is simply to hide someone else's fear.

So, toxicity leads to selfish behaviour
Designed to protect
Some vulnerability.
A vulnerability that is usually hidden
From all involved in the sorry situation.

Until that vulnerability is recognised and faced
The fear will still persist
And so too will the toxicity
Be it either thought or behaviour or both.

It is hard to face fears
And much easier
To deny them.
So no wonder
So many people
Continue to suffer
Whichever side of the toxicity
They are on.

Endurance

For a new identity to endure
It requires us to stand firm
In our new beliefs
Our new attitude
Our new identity.

This may be easier said than done.
Not only is our new self
Taking some getting used to
We may find those around us
Challenging us
Doubting our validity
Testing our credibility.
Some may even resort to ridicule
To get us back onside
Into the fold
Where we behave predictably
According to their rules.

This is to be expected
If we wish to change ourselves
To become more of ourselves.
To feel more comfortable in our own skins
Rather than the skin
Required of us by others.

It is easy to let fears
Get the better of us
As we are so very tempted
To people-please once again.

It is why lasting change
Is so hard to achieve
As it requires us
To stand firm enough
In our convictions
To let criticism and ridicule
Slide off around us
Like the water cascading off
The feathers
Of the proverbial duck's back.

Yes, but ...

No-one can help a yes-butter.
It is like hitting your head
Against the proverbial brick wall.
All your suggestions will require a change
Of attitude at the very least
And most often will require a change
Of very much more than that.

Don't waste your breath!
A yes-butter's attention
Will stubbornly stop at mention of change
And how impossible that change
Will be to embrace
Because of this or that or whatever else.

Short of a miracle nothing will help
And even miracles require a fully open mind.
So, in short, until fear of change
Is tackled head on
Any advice, however good
Is destined to fall on deaf ears.

The response of 'yes, but'
Will be on repeat
And you can only listen to a finite number of those
Before your energy wilts
And your good nature is threatened!

Be kind to yourself and admit defeat
As, unfortunately, whatever you say
That brick wall isn't going to go away
Any time soon.

Wordsmith

It is not what is said that matters
As words can hide a multitude.
It is what is done that matters.
Does it match
Or are the words simply proved to be a sham?
That is the real test.

A wordsmith is skilled
At creating a truth
Whether it is really true or not.
So look at what happens
On a day-to-day basis
And base your appraisal on that.

Not What It Seems

All are equally worthy
Equally important
Equally significant.

What screws it all up
Are the fears
Of quite a significant number
Who then protect themselves
By pushing others down
And trying to ignore them completely.
They may even wish to eradicate
Those from their lives
Who threaten to trigger
Their prejudices
And intolerance.

Such behaviour
Is not about others
As they believe it is.
It is simply about themselves
Their very own deeply hidden
And totally unacknowledged
Fears and vulnerability.

Indulgence

Does someone accept you for who you are
However wayward your point of view?

Or do they simply indulge you?
You will see sense eventually.

And in the meantime
They allow you to embarrass yourself
To expose your fanciful thinking
Until you capitulate to their superior knowledge.
Until you see sense
Which, of course, you will do
If they've got anything to do with it!

Evil

I do not believe in evil people
But I do believe in
Profoundly damaged people
Who therefore make evil choices.
It is not the same thing
Though the end result is.

Such evil choices will not be changed
Until that person sees a need to change them.
You cannot expect a change to happen
In any other way.
So, spend your energy protecting yourself
As that you can and must do.

Have You Lost Your Mind?

No, but I do listen to my heart.

A Serious Business

Is life an oh-so serious business?
Are you afraid that if you have fun
Take your eye off the ball
Take your hands off the controls
Indulge and enjoy yourself
That somehow it will all come crashing down?
Do you believe that success
Requires a strictness
A dedication that leaves no room for joy?
Do you frown upon those who fling cares aside
And laugh and dance and sing
Who appear to treat life so very, very glibly
Without the due care and attention it deserves?

Does their world fall apart
Do they suffer appalling retribution
Do they live to regret their moments of joy
Or do they seem to get off scot-free?
Does it seem so unfair that they can have fun
Whilst you spend your time
Holding so much together?

Why not promise yourself a bit of that fun
Kick over the traces
Without the guilt or the shame or the fear of doom?
And see whether catastrophe does manifest
Or whether, God forbid, life still runs quite smoothly
Even without you at the helm.

Mind Control

My mind is self-important
So deems itself to be
The ultimate arbiter of this verse that I write.
I have struggled and striven to obey my mind's rules
In the hope that my mind
Really does know what's best.

But too frequently I find
To my complete disappointment
That I feel only frustration
And am underwhelmed instead.
In fact to the point that I often delete
The whole and complete fricking thing!

And so, I just wait … and the wait isn't long
For a verse to just pop into my head.
Though, memo to me, please remember don't ask
For my mind's very vocal opinion on that!

Once a version of the verse is completely complete
My mind then does muscle in.
It wants to improve but more often than not
I find it dilutes, even ruins in fact
The intended and genuine message.

My mind wants me to people-please
To be up to some standard
To be mindful of expectations.

But expectations are … well … something expected
So no new surprises forthcoming in that!

How does one smash the so well-established
Exceed, move on, even move up a notch?

Well, that requires some risk
And trust in whatever it is that feels right.
And, equally important, it might be despite
Whatever the mind's
Opinions on that!

Still Connected

Let the connection be what it is
There but not there
Essential but not essential
Enduring
A part of life in its broadest sense.

It cannot be grasped
It cannot be denied
It just is.

It is meaningful
It is meaningless
It is what it is.

It defies description
It defies logic
It refuses to go away.

It hovers beyond the edge of understanding
An essence, but of what
Is the question.

As understanding is impossible
Acceptance is all that is left.
Simple acceptance
That whatever it is, now it is not.

Let it endure as a memory
And a wonderful memory at that!
Then get on with life
No more longing, no more waiting
And most importantly
Let go of the baggage.

Too Old!

Age is irrelevant
Unless we listen to our egos
Always harking back to the past
And lamenting its absence
In our present.

Our hearts, our feelings
Have no regard for age.
We say we don't feel our age
Well, why might that be so
Because feelings are not governed
By age perhaps?

We say someone is
So young at heart
All the more reason
To listen to our hearts
To be led by our hearts
Age be damned!

We are never too old to change
Unless we need an excuse
To close our ears
To what our hearts are telling us …

So, you were saying you were too old
For what?

More Alive

Do not make choices out of fear
Of the possible consequences.
Make a choice out of a desire
Because it makes you feel
More alive, more excited
More pleased to be living your life.

Fears That Do Not Exist

Does your comfort
Your degree of security
Rely on your understanding
Your knowing how things work
How they will work?
Do they rely on predictability
On knowing exactly where you are going
Ahead of actually going there?

But if such is the case
We are very different.
I find my greatest peace of mind
Comes when I trust that all will be well.

I find it is distrust
Feeling that life could not possibly go well
Without strict controls
Without strict rules
Without strict guidance
To ensure some aim is reached
That introduces fears for my future.
Fears that simply do not exist
If I am willing to trust
That all will be well.

Especially if I stop getting in my way
By thinking that I know best!

Beyond the Mind

You're stuck, you're frustrated!
So, you dwell
You reflect
You contemplate
But nothing of significance springs to mind
To release the frustration
To unstick yourself.
And that is because
It is necessary to go somewhat deeper
To go beyond the mind.

Only by going deep into your feelings
Can you hope to see what it is
That is so within grasp
But which stubbornly so far
Has stayed completely hidden from view.
And if your mind keeps strangling feelings
Well, no wonder you end up stuck.
Because frustration is a feeling that's thwarted
By the strict control of the limiting mind.

And being able to see that that is the case
Is a very necessary requirement
Before you can contemplate
Going sufficiently deep
To really get unstuck
By going beyond the mind.

Doing Nothing

For all too many of us
It is just too hard
To simply do nothing ...

To be vacant
To be still
To stop doing
To stop thinking
To let ourselves drift
Without a care in the world
Aimlessly
Letting the world just pass us by
With an empty mind
Letting go and relaxing
With no sense of guilt.

Many may not see the point
Of just doing nothing.
What a waste of such valuable time!
A time when so much can be achieved
Boxes ticked
To-do lists tackled.
Time enough for such indulgences
When goals are reached
When success is well and truly under our belts.

But then
When are our ultimate goals ever truly reached?
We constantly strive to do better
Be better
Achieve more.
And that luxury
Of doing nothing
Of just letting time pass
Retreats further and further
Over the horizon
A point never to be reached
In a lifetime of doing.

All the more reason I say
To take our indulgences now
Not waiting for some
Unspecified time in the future
Which, as I have already said
Is a time
That will never come to pass.

And remember
Doing nothing requires practice.
It requires you to give yourself permission
To keep practising
Until it becomes as easy as doing.

The Messenger

What if our bodies are messengers
Ones to which we just don't listen?
Their failings bearing hidden messages
So clear if we take the time to hear.

Bad backs breaking under the burdens we bear.
High blood pressure as we constantly
Push ourselves to stay in control.
Bad knees as we feel pulled
Both this way and that.
Bad teeth as we zip our lips
To take care that we don't, even accidentally
Blurt out our real truth.
I could go on but you get the drift.

Then, a major ignorance on our part
Would be failing to listen to our body.
It suffers in silence as our minds take control
Until it breaks from being so misunderstood
So sidelined and swamped
By the mind's self-importance.

If such is the case
We must look to ourselves
If we are to find the ultimate cure.
But our minds will demand that
It is others who cure us
Preferably by yesterday!

But what if we need to do our bit too
By listening to our body?
To hear the messages
Hidden in the ailments
Rather than allowing our self-important
And fearful minds
To completely run the show.

Catching Up

Physics is the science of form
But as physics evolves
And explores even further
It finds it must embrace
The world of the formless.

So, scientists
With their strictly rational minds
Are finding themselves straying
Into the world of the formless.
They are grappling with
The conundrums
Of the world not being
As they believed it to be
Having refused such a possibility
In the past!

So, is it masculines
With their strictly rational minds
Who will succeed
In being believed
As they expose the world of the formless?
A world with which feminines
Have long been familiar
Without needing any so-called proof
Because
They just knew that it worked.

But they were not then believed
Because their knowledge
Was unproved
And therefore was not to be trusted.

We feminines look on
With our knowing
As masculines strive to catch up.

They must prove it to themselves
And claim all the glory
Rather than believing and trusting
In feminine knowing
Which is still way ahead of the science
Way ahead of the strictly limited rational mind.

Form & Formless

Dwelling in the overlap
Of a Venn diagram
Where the circle of form
And the circle of the formless
Overlap.

A masculine excels in a world of form
A feminine excels in a world of the formless.
It is possible to live in this world of form
With no feminine skills at all
As indeed do so many people.

It is almost impossible though
To live in this world of form
With no masculine skills
Without becoming a hermit.
To be one who lives beyond the mind
Where the formless and deep knowing are to be found.

We have a form; the world is form
But deep knowing is found in the formless.
So all of us would certainly benefit
From successfully tapping into
And learning how to combine
Both masculine and feminine skills.

To successfully combine the form and formless
In a way that brings wisdom
And meaning to life in form
Without having to wait for the death of form
In order to know the meaning of life.

The Measure of a Life

Are you happy and joyful
Loving your life?
Are you content
At peace with yourself?

I don't ask the question
'What is it you do?'
I ask how you feel about
What you are doing.

Your life may be lived
At a great rate of knots
Or placidly
Playfully enjoying backwaters.
Either way requires you to feel good about your feelings
If you are to feel fulfilled.

Food for Thought

Seeing things through the fresh eyes of a new identity.

Discernment

Discernment is about choosing wisely.
It does not require judgement
An assessment of good or bad.
It simply requires that a choice be made
According to what feels to be
To each individual one of us
Completely right in the moment.

For that very reason
It may not be a rational choice
According to anyone else!
For what feels right is for you to decide
No explanation ever being required.

Winning

You cannot fight and beat a seasoned fighter
One whose aim is to win
Whatever the cost.
Unless of course
You are, yourself
A seasoned fighter
For whom fighting is your raison d'être.

So, if you cannot win by fighting
Does that mean you cannot win?
No.
You can win by rising above it
Making the fighter
Completely irrelevant in your life
A waste of your time
A waste of your attention
Not worthy of consideration.
It is discombobulating
It is the unexpected ploy.

How can you ignore them?
How *dare* you ignore them!
Take it from me
It gets easier with time
Until they no longer impact
Upon your life
Until they hold no power over you.
And that is winning in my book.

Going Without

If we feel we are going without
It is time to look at the harder choices
Those that take us
Outside of our comfort zone
Into the unknown
Where there are no guarantees.

To feel a sense of achievement, not paucity
We need to be brave
To have the courage
To change things up.

It is as easy and as hard as that!

Lady Luck

Are you tempted to say that
They've had a luckier life than me
They've just not had it so bad?

Whatever the truth of their life
Which you do not know for sure
It is a good excuse for you to believe
That you have drawn the shorter straw
In order to justify
At least in your mind
Why, for you to make your life
As good as theirs
Is just too big an ask.

But it is just an excuse you know
It is not the reason you think it is.

Enough

The surest way of not having enough
Is to fear that we do not have enough!

Whatever we have will never be enough
Unless we acknowledge and get rid of that fear
Which prevents us from seeing when what we have got
Is actually quite plenty enough.

Failed, or Yet to Succeed?

If something is not working out
Or if something that used to work stops working
We are taught to believe we have failed.
We are judged so often by others
As having failed
As having got it wrong
Of somehow being wanting.

We may be deemed wanting
In our ability to stick at it
To carry on despite the odds.
Or we may be deemed as foolish
For having embarked on such an endeavour
In the very first place.
We may even be deeming ourselves
As having been wanting or foolish.

We see others making a success
At what we have so miserably
Failed to achieve for ourselves
Rubbing salt in the wound
That already promises to fester
On and on …
However much we wish it would not.

It makes us so wary of trying our hand
At anything with no guarantee of success.
And how limiting is that
When guaranteeing anything in life
Is so very hard to do?

So, we end up playing it safe
By never taking a risk
Or not moving on when really we should.
Anything to avoid the shame of failure
In the eyes of others as well as our own.

But what if we stop seeing 'not working' as 'failed'
And see it as 'yet to succeed'?
Then allow ourselves to reassess
To learn from what does not work
And learn to try something else instead.

To consider it all just part of the path
To discovering what really does work.
And to not give up but to be seen as having strength
By not being cowed
Because we are not there yet
Because we have yet to succeed.

Dredging Up the Past

How do we reminisce about the past?
Do we remember it as good
Or do we remember it as bad?
What if we are not remembering it at all
But remembering only
A version of the past
That suits our needs?

Could we not bear to think
That the past was not as good
As we would have liked
So the rose-tinted spectacles
Are firmly in place?
Or do we need to feed our anger
Our rage, our guilt about some
Self-identified hurt to ourselves or another?

Hm, tricky questions both
But neither may be worth answering
When we throw into the mix
Why do we need to waste our present
By re-living any version of the past?

Life is for living now.
You are no longer that person
Who lived in the past
So why keep dredging up memories
About a person who no longer exists?

Empowerment

Empowerment is not about
Losing our fears.
It is about recognising them
And learning how to do
Something about them.

We will always
Need to deal with our fears
But we can become experts
In how to go about that!

Hope

Why is hope so important
So integral to our lives?
Because hope uplifts
It is the light at the end of the tunnel.

Hope is a future worth living
So never be without it!
And please never
Take away anyone else's hope
Because who are you to know anyone's future?
And that includes your own!

So many times
We are tempted to lose hope
To believe in the worst
That we cannot overcome
Whatever it is
That challenges us
Because it is just too big.

But, by doing that
We are claiming to know the future
And put like that it is rather ridiculous
At least for those of us
Without second sight.

A lack of hope squeezes out
Any chance of the new.

A new that may be quite different
But can still be rewarding
Provided we are prepared
To give it a go.

So, believe in your future
Whatever it might be.
Take it one step at a time
Enjoy the small things
And bide time
For something more
To come your way
In whatever form that may be.

You may have to watch quite closely
For that something more in your life
And may need to let go
Of your expectations
Of what your life is meant to be.

The past is the past
But the future is still blank.
Fill it with whatever feels good.
If you search deep enough
You will find something that's good.
Let that be your focus
And then take it from there
Keeping hope alive in your life.

Leaps of Faith

If you wait for big decisions
To become less hard to make
Then you are waiting in vain.

Life on pause
Treading water
Holding breath
Imagining life falling into place
Without having to step
Outside of your comfort zone
Into the as yet unknown …
Which, of course, would require trust.

Yes, trust is essential
If change is ever to happen.
Leaps of faith
Where fear must be overcome.

Then, and only then
Will life blossom and grow.
Be brave, you do deserve that change
Because that is what a rich life
Is very much about.

Castles in the Air

We say something is
'Too good to be true'
And indeed if someone's ego is involved
Then such is most likely the case!

But what if something good
Is actually true?
We doubt it, we dismiss it
We wait for the other shoe to drop.
We don't believe in
Such synchronicity
Such strokes of good fortune.
We call it too bizarre to be real
We are just fantasising
Building castles in the air …

Why do we squash such hopes
Call them completely impossible
Just figments of our imagination
Instead of believing in our luck?

Is it why so many of us
Are stuck in a rut?
Dismissing our luck
For fear of being ridiculed
Accused of believing fantasy
Of building castles in the air.

A Healthy Balance

It is not an either-or
But it is a healthy balance.
A balance that is unique
To each and every one of us.

Our femininity is about
Listening to our hearts
To be guided by our feelings
And requires us first to recognise
What it is we actually feel.
Best done through
Quiet contemplation
And then standing strong
As we proceed to act accordingly.

It is this action that requires
A masculine approach.
And so without our masculinity
We are full of ideas
Of dreams, of intentions
That spring from our hearts
But they fail to come to life.

So, finding the feminine within us
Does not supplant the masculine.
Finding the masculine within us
Does not supplant the feminine.

Either without the other
Is equally limiting
By making us less happy and less successful.

The purpose of the internal feminine
Is to help the internal masculine
To work in a way
That brings joy and happiness
Instead of domination and conflict.

The purpose of the internal masculine
Is to help the internal feminine
Persist in their work
So ideas and intentions
Can successfully be brought to fruition.

In short
The feminine excels
In the truly creative
The masculine is essential
In bringing such creations to life.

So, why not strive to be both
In some shape or form
If you desire a life
That is both happy
And successful?

About the Author

It is a great temptation to write about my past life as is customary here. However, as it is just that, my past life, it bears no relevance to who I am now, so would simply be misleading!

I also find that I do not need to validate myself by talking about my past achievements, and would hope that someone would not think the less of me for not doing so.

As, by the time you read this, I may have continued to change my life, there is little point in giving you any information about my current circumstances either.

I do not wish to become attached to any version of me, so I apologise if this disappoints you.

Acknowledgements

My life continues to be a great source of inspiration for my verses.

All the people I meet or come across, those who unfailingly support me or those who are intent on challenging me, are potential triggers for a new verse.

I therefore thank everyone who touches my life. Your presence is essential to my growth. Everything serves to make me stronger and more confident, whether that be the easy way or the hard way. It doesn't matter which!

Index

Milton Keynes UK
Ingram Content Group UK Ltd.
UKHW041903120324
439302UK00005B/254